Phases

PRAISE FOR *PHASES*
BY BELINDA BETKER

"Belinda Betker's first collection of poetry, Phases, is a captivating tribute to the lunar and life cycles. Fierce and richly erotic, with acuity and candour her poems shine a bright light onto an intimate world and burst with power and play. Both lovingly tender and don't-mess-with-me tough, Betker's is an empowering voice." – **Sandra Ridley, Griffin Prize finalist for *Silvija***

"'Walk loose,' writes Belinda Betker in this riveting collection, 'take up space like you own it.' And oh, how she does. These bold, tender, cocky, shy, hilarious, heart-breaking poems enter a room like they own the house. Phases is a must-read and so you must. This is a beautifully nuanced voice that dares, teases, and challenges all notions of gender. I can think of few poets who do so with such generosity." – **Katherine Lawrence, award-winning poet and author**

"Belinda Betker's debut poetry collection, Phases, is a significant contribution to LGBTQ2S+ literature. The collection explores the trials of a lifelong journey toward knowing—toward identity—and the wayfinding power of embracing the body's sensual nature... The poems... lean intimately into moments of great vulnerability and great strength. As a reader, I am grateful for the discrete and sustained attention she has brought to each poem, breathing through the pain toward a 'place of knowing.'" – **Clea Roberts, *The Humber Literary Review***

"In Phases, Betker traces the transition of sexual identity through marriage, 'coming out,' and drag persona. Gritty, funny, eloquent and most definitely relevant." – **Judges, Creative Saskatchewan Publishing Award, 2020 Saskatchewan Book Awards (Finalist)**

"An honest look at the fluidity of the self, Phases *pushes back against normative expectations of gender and sexuality in a series of poems that's both deft and defiant. Belinda Betker, also known as Dyke van Dick, is an uncompromising cultural observer, the perfect guide to warn readers against past mistakes and renew their faith in the future. The poems in* Phases *are bona-fide manifestos, and a must read for those interested in how to live well in the 21st century."* – **Judges, SK Arts Poetry Award Honouring Anne Szumigalski, 2020 Saskatchewan Book Awards (Finalist)**

"These poems are at once tender and shy, cocksure and sassy, like the many faces that appear here in all their phases: childhood, young womanhood, motherhood—not to mention middle-age drag kinghood! In these pages, to be a woman manfully is just another way to be, and beauty is in the eye of the beheld." – **Elizabeth Philips, award-winning author of *Torch River* and *The Afterlife of Birds***

Phases

Poetry
by
Belinda Betker

SHADOWPAW PRESS *Reprise*

PHASES

By Belinda Betker

Second Edition
Revised and expanded by the author
Published 2022 by
Shadowpaw Press Reprise
Regina, Saskatchewan, Canada
www.shadowpawpress.com

First edition published 2019
by Coteau Books

Trade Paperback ISBN: 978-1-989398-44-9
Ebook ISBN: 978-1-989398-45-6

Cover design by Jamie Marie Olson
Interior design by Edward Willett

*For all my families,
everywhere they are*

TABLE OF CONTENTS

Just like the moon, I go through phases
tattoo

1

Saros Cycle

As far as I'm concerned, being any gender is a drag.
Patti Smith

⟩⟩⟩⟩● Girls and Boys When I'm Five

Mom and I are girls,
and Dad and my brothers are boys.
Girls have vee-gees,
and boys have pee-pees.

Girls wear panties and dresses,
and boys wear underpants and jeans.
Moms are housewives,
and dads have jobs.

Girls help moms make beds, wash
dishes and clothes, sweep floors
and vacuum, and make pickles in jars,
and boys play catch with dads.

Girls play with dolls and Barbies,
and look after brothers
who play Lego, toy cars, guns,
and cowboys and Indians.

Girls grow up and get married
and have kids, and boys grow up
and get jobs and get married
and buy cars and trailers and boats.

Girls get really old and grey
and wrinkled and become grandmas,
and boys become whiskered grandpas,
and then they all die.

ⰥⰥⰥⰥ● **Out of the Box**

Flip-top box, sixty-four colours,
but I'm only allowed one

for faces, arms, and legs—
no goldenrod, Indian red, raw sienna;
no mahogany, copper, or umber;
no colours of the rainbow.

Just this one, says Teacher
as she hands me a crayon
called flesh—no other shades
permitted for skin.

Her hand over mine
moves the crayon in little circles.
See! It's easier
to stay inside the lines
when you round up to the edges
rather than trying to colour straight.

3

›››››●**Beaten**

I rub my bruised thighs
under the dinner table.

Is it safe to say anything
about Jim from Grade 8,
who shoves me down,
kicks and hits me almost every day,

no matter how soon I rush out the door
of my Grade 3 classroom,
or dilly-dally in the hallway,
or which route I take home?

Mom talks about morning coffee klatch.
Dad complains about the blockheads
at work, while my two brothers make faces
at each other. I blurt,
A guy at school
beats me up after class.

Dad drums his fingers
by his emptied plate.
          What do you do
          to make him mad?
          Just stay out of his way.

He raises his evening paper, snaps
it open. No one else says anything.
It's my turn to clear the table, wash
dishes, my stomach tight
against the counter's edge.

PHASES

⟩⟩⟩⟩● Drum a Beat

My fingers *tap tap tap*
my thighs
under the table,

pat pat pat, forefinger
on forefinger,
beat beat beat of my pulse.

We've got a secret,
Richard and I—
we're getting married

when we grow up
and he's famous
like Ringo.

Drum drum drum
of the rhythms
we beat on paint cans

after men leave
their days' work
building new houses

at the end of our street—
an off-limits area
where we play every day.

Knock knock knock
on the door when Richard
comes by to walk me to school.

Thump thump thump
of my heart
as he walks me home.

No one from school
beats beats beats
me up anymore.

⟩⟩⟩⟩●Three Musketeers

Richard makes friends with Danny,
and Danny likes me, too.
He's the cutest guy in Grade 3
and the coolest guy in our school.

We call each other Musketeers,
all for one and one for all.
Or I'm Wonder Woman, and they're Supermen,
or we shoot marbles or play ball.

The best thing is, they're my best friends,
we suit each other to a tee.
And just as cool, they're my bodyguards—
no one dares to bully me.

⟩⟩⟩⟩● Dress Up

Mom's favourite skirt,
brown-sugared wool—rick-rack
and embroidery loop a traceable path
'round and 'round the flaring hem.

Her favourite blouse, satiny white—
Cute tomata! printed between
winking red tomato faces.
Gleaming pearl buttons fasten
the front and three-quarter-length sleeves.

I button her top over my chest, flat profile
in the sliding closet-door mirrors,

gyrate my hips to swish
the skirt's hula-hoop fullness.

Dad's side of the closet—
his shirt sleeves dangle from the ends
of my arms, ties reach my knees,
his prized snap-brim hat
covers my face.

Years later, my mother remakes
her skirt into a hassock cover,
but her blouse hangs in the back
of my out-of-season closet,

while Dad's hat rests
on the highest shelf
in a dust-free box.

⟩⟩⟩⟩● Sleight of Hand

I see the purse
in downtown Woolworths—
a beige clutch, wrist strap,
sliding silver closure.
I swing it by my side,
imagine it holding
all my coins and dollar bills,
my cat's eye marbles,
and the miniature treasure chest
from this morning's
Cap'N Crunch cereal.

I wonder how many allowances
it will take to own it
even as I imagine Sister Agatha's voice,
Thou shalt not covet.

Dad startles me.
       What are you doing
       with that purse?
I slide it off my wrist, shove it back
in the display bin.
I'm going to save up for it, I say.
       Well, we're leaving now.
       Go catch up with your mother.

I daydream about the purse in the car
on the way home, still think about it
when I help Mom unpack the shopping bags.

In one of them is the purse, and Dad smiles.
       It's yours.
I've never gotten a present before
for no reason.
       Mom says, *You've got your dad*
       wrapped around your little finger,
but I don't know what that means.

I swing my purse on my wrist,
wiggle my fingers, wave my hand,
wonder how this magic happened.

))))●What I Know

It happens to goldfish in glass bowls:
too much food, or not enough—
belly up
means flush them down.

It happens to earthworms,
slashed in half
with kitchen knives.
Neighbour boys focus
pinpoints of sun
through magnifying glasses
over the writhing pieces.

It happens to Grandpa—
Mom home from the hospital
on Tuesday afternoon, incoherent,

choking with tears.
At ten, all I know is his heart
has broken hers.

⟩⟩⟩⟩● First Funeral

I never saw him
with his eyes closed,

but everyone's relieved
Grandpa looks like he's sleeping.

Yet the incense, too strong,
church, too hot,
mass, too long—
I sink to my knees.

Outside, an aunt says
I'm her favourite—
she's glad to be with me
for some fresh air.

But later, I overhear
her tell other relatives
in the living room—
       What a shame!
       She used to be such a cute kid,
       but now look at her—those buck teeth
       and glasses, her blotchy skin.

I sink to my knees.

>>>>● **Flattened**

My Saturday chore
after Mom and Dad grocery shop—
flatten, fold, and crease
paper bags into thirds.

But the bags keep unfolding
until I sit on them, add bag by bag
to the stack, flattened together.
I slide the whole pile neatly on edge
into a storage bag,

pleased with how smart I am,
but my brother laughs.
      That works 'cuz you're fat!
And my other brother says,
      Not only fat, but flat and ugly,
and Mom yells, *That's enough.*

I race to my room, too upset now
to play with Millie the Model paper dolls
or Heavenly Blue Wedding cut-outs.

Fat, flat, and ugly
means I'll never be Millie, never
be a bride.

⟩⟩⟩⟩● My Turn

It was never my brothers' turn,
always mine, to peel and cut
potatoes, peel and chop
carrots, peel myself away
from *Bewitched* to help Mom make supper.

Then it was my turn
to clear and wipe the table,
put away leftovers, sweep the floor,
wash the dishes while my brothers
argued whose turn it was to dry.

Afterwards, they'd rush off
to watch *Gilligan's Island* or *Gunsmoke*,
while I helped Mom bathe my baby brother,
dress him in footed pyjamas,

warm his bottle, feed him, rock him
to sleep while I practised
twitching my nose.

⟩⟩⟩⟩● Francis/Frances

Mr. H. announces
a new classmate will start Friday.
For two days, we ask, over and over,
Girl or boy? Boy or girl?

Mr. H. finally gives in:
>   *The student's name*
>   *is pronounced Francis,*
which increases the flurry
of our wondering

until Friday, when Frances
hunches in, long, straight black hair
screening her dark eyes.

There's something different
about this new girl I can't pinpoint
as we whisper amongst ourselves.

Helen hisses,
>   *She's an Indian.*
What do you mean? I ask.
>   *You know—a wagon-burner*, she says.

I've never heard *wagon-burner* before
but write it in a note to Linda
that Mr. H. intercepts.

My after-school detentions
become a week of history lessons
I never forget.

⟩⟩⟩⟩●A Doctor Talks to 9-to-12-year-olds

The small blue booklet—
my initiation
into what's coming—
jeans and striped t-shirts
exchanged for dresses, chafe
of bras, self-conscious
shift of thick sanitary napkins
looped into an awkward elastic belt
inside my panties.

Boys at school
refuse to let me play
football, sneak up
behind me, snap
my bra straps, elbow each other, jeer
my boobs, tits, knockers—

mimic how I walk funny
once a month.

))))● **Elephant**

How do you know an elephant
has her period?

There's a dime on your dresser
and your mattress is gone.

Funny when a girl says it—
embarrassing when a boy does.

There's nothing the doctor
wrote in the booklet

that tells me
how to deal with that.

⟩⟩⟩⟩● Grade 6

The coolest girl in class
mouths a silent message
to me across the rows.

I shrug, raise my hands
mime, *What?*
She puckers
her cherry-glossed lips
into slow exaggerated
silent pronunciation,
but I can't make out
what she means.

What would it take
to understand her unvoiced words,
to comprehend my desire
to decipher
her mouth and lips?

ᲒᲒᲒᲒᲒ●Good Girl

Mr. L. walks so quietly
between the rows
during Creative Writing
I forget he's there
until he punches
his signet ring down
onto the crown of my head
as I bend over the folded note

just passed to me. It's addressed and signed
with symbols we girls design at recess
or after school at each other's houses,
unique logos for each of us
so anyone not-in-the-know
won't know who notes are to or from,

but Mr. L knew he was the *Mr. Snotface*
in the note. So, it was me he kept
after school in detention
for his self-described heart-to-heart
about how I should follow the rules,
write creatively as assigned,
not pass notes,
and be a good girl—
all the while staring at my chest.

⟩⟩⟩⟩● Night Light

Nothing bad ever happens
when the moon shines in
the wide uncurtained windows—
my childhood bedroom.

Freight trains grumble
through the dark.

Miles away,
the perpetual sweep
of the airport's single spotlight
splays across the cloud-pocked sky.

But moonless nights
can't be trusted—

fumbling beneath the covers—
nothing safe to touch.

⟩⟩⟩⟩● Big Ethel, Grade 9

Hey, bucky—
bucky bucky beaver,
hey, gopher,
hey, Bugs Bunny.
Hey, wabbit—
bet you eat corn
through a picket fence
with those teeth.

Hey, Bugs Bunny,
Hey, Big Ethel—
oh wait, you've got pimples
and thick glasses, so, yeah,
you're kinda like Big Ethel, only uglier.

Hey, wabbit, hey, gopher,
c'mon, let's see a smile.
Whoops, no, never mind.
Forget that—you're too gross,
too ugly,
bucky bucky beaver.

Go fuck yourself, I finally say,
no one else will,
you pencil-prick
useless dick,
as I toss a pencil stub
at him. His friends laugh
every time I drop other pencils
beside him at his desk or locker—

he soon figures out
to leave me alone.

⟩⟩⟩⟩● Mixed Signals 1972

Daisy petals picked
and discarded. *Love me,*
love me not.

Initials penned within hearts
inside the back page
of every Hilroy notebook.

Wasted evenings pretending
not to yearn for his call, endless

wait when my mother dials out
just when he might phone me,
get the busy signal, lose
his nerve, and never try again.

That's what I tell myself,
long past midnight, tear-sopped
tissues, torn-up
paper hearts—

the what-ifs and maybes,
second-guessing
his teasing smile
outside French class—
that morning wink.

⟩⟩⟩⟩◐ Hit the Beach

I buy blue stretch denim
and a pattern for a two-piece bathing suit,
  Suitably modest, Mom says
  so it won't show too much—

but showing is what I want, like the girls
in bikinis I admire from the shade
near the shore at Lac Ste. Anne.
I hunch over my book, too self-conscious
in my homemade bathing suit
to even walk to the water.

A few weeks later,
I see what I really want
in the Sears Days sale flyer.

I regard myself that afternoon
in my bedroom's full-length mirror.
It's a little bit itsy-bitsy
teensy-weeny, I think,
admiring my new blue-and-white
polka-dot bikini,

eager for the new me
to hit the beach.

⟩⟩⟩⟩● **Savasana**

I wake at home
on my back—

a starfish corpse
on flannelette,

obsessed about
What if? How will I?
when my belly cramps,
shooting pain. I stifle my cries
so my family won't hear.

"I'm Eighteen" and other
Alice Cooper songs from *Killer*
play over and over in my mind.

A half-hour later,
blood oozes
into the toilet—

a tiny sac dangles
from inside me, swings
slow arcs. I pull
it from myself, gently—
no longer knowing
who or what
I am.

))))● Blood

I prayed for it
despite no longer believing
in prayer—

but bleeding frees me
to march to his locker,
where he sniggers, elbowing
his pals as I storm up,

his sneer jolting to shock
as I splatter a gush
of obscenities

that prompts his friends
to mock the brute
instead of me.

Striding away, my stomps
match the pounding of my heart,
but outside, the sun
gentles my face. I catch

my breath, look forward
to tomorrow's forecast—
bright, cloudless skies.

⟩⟩⟩⟩●Tied Right

I could tie a double Windsor
better than any of them,
with or without a mirror,

on myself, or someone else—
my talent for knots
and entanglements.

All the guys and gals
in my Naval Reserve division
wanted me
to tie their ties—

work dress, parade uniform,
marching in military rhythm:
      Parade—atten-shun!
      Parade—right march!
      Parade—about face!
      Eyes right!
      Parade halt!
      Right dress!

⟩⟩⟩)●Cherry Whisky

My girlfriends are jealous.
My boyfriend
is better than theirs—
mine's older, mine works, mine owns a car.

Noontime, he picks me up, drives
us to the Royal Canadian Legion in Nutana,
where we have a liquid lunch—
legal because we're Reservists
with Department of National Defence IDs.

I pretend I have a spare after lunch,
skip Grade 12 Chemistry for another few
cherry-whisky-and-7s,
return to school, giddy, just in time

for English class. Mr. C. calls on me
to analyze today's poem.
Does he know I'm drunk?
Does he know I think he is, too?

Doug waits across the street
after English, parks us at the weir
to watch the submarine races
until there's just enough time
before his bartending shift
at the Sheraton Cavalier
to get me home. When Doug drops
me off, Dad says,
        You're wasting your time
        with that guy

and scowls even harder at Christmas
when Doug's gift to me is an oversized stuffed bear
with attached heart-shaped tag—
Here's a huggable, squeezable, kissable, lovable Panda
for huggable, squeezable, kissable, lovable you,

but I don't tell about the gift
I already let Doug unwrap,
unbutton, unlace.

25

⟩⟩⟩⟩● Point Pleasant Park

Halifax felt as far away
as I could possibly get
from Saskatoon—
my first military posting
after high-school graduation.

No room that summer
in the women's barracks on base
for all the female Reservists
from across the county.
I was posted instead into campus dorms
at St. Mary's University.

No supervisors or chaperones on site
or in sight, my new roommate, Mary, and I
sit on the floor at a dorm party
on either side of a cute guy
with tanned skin, a Reg Force sailor.

What did we talk about
besides where we were from,
our respective trades,
before I noticed a glinting line
edging the bottom of his pants.
Really? Staples? I asked, then offered
to properly hem his brown corduroys.

The next day, we walked hand in hand
to Point Pleasant Park—
trails through the woods, a Martello tower,
ruins of old forts, a huge anchor monument
along Sailor's Memorial Way.

We rolled up our jeans, held hands again
during my first walk in the Atlantic Ocean,
while I wondered whether today
would someday become a pleasant memory.

PHASES

⟩⟩⟩⟩● Queensland Beach, Nova Scotia

We night-shifters rumble
on a DND bus down the backwoods road
from the Communications Centre
to Base Quarters and breakfast,

crowding afterwards
into Stormin' Norman's van
to go to Queensland Beach.

We alternately bodysurf, sleep
on beach towels, and splash in the ocean
until late afternoon's return to base.

Shower's sting afterwards—
sun-sanded skin, my eyelids
so badly burned it scalded to blink
as I squinted through dinner
of scallops, lobster,
summer peas and carrots
before busing back up the hill
to our next shift.

I was one of only a half-dozen
female Reservists on base, getting paid
to learn a trade, spending days at the beach, partying
on weekends, blooming from as much male attention
as I could ever have wanted, treated like a queen—

oh, those nineteen-year-old hormones
and free birth control. If only I'd known
how remarkable it was to be that carefree,
that young, that in the moment.

⟩⟩⟩⟩● Red Wings

East-coast evening, carousing
on the clubroom patio, mood lighting
set by burning moonshine alcohol
in metal ashtrays.

Later, Henri keeps a lookout
while I sneak in
to the off-limits men's barracks,
slip naked into his bed.

    This night is all for you,
he murmurs, head between my legs.

Afterwards, he comes back to bed,
turns on the small bedside lamp,
offers me a small towel
as he wipes a damp facecloth
across his blood-smeared lips.

I'm horrified, apologize.
I didn't know my period would start.

    Don't be embarrassed, he says,
    I don't know about your guys
    back home, but here, red wings
    are a badge of honour.

⟩⟩⟩⟩● Tattoos

Fully rigged sailing ship inked
on his lower right forearm—
the first tattoo I ever touched
on a man's skin.

A bit cliché, a sailor and a ship,
but a few years after
Hurricane Blanche's destruction in Halifax
during CFDR's endless summer of '75
and 1976's east-coast posting, I transferred
permanently to Victoria, moved in,
and married him at City Hall.

Each deployment, another tattoo.
He returned after two months
at sea, proud to show off
the griffin on his right bicep.

Are you sure? I asked, scrutinizing
the crimson, reared-up stallion—
small wings, a centre horn
projected from its forehead.
        Of course, I'm sure, he sneered,
            everyone knows what a griffin looks like,
but I pondered mythological creatures—
checked our *Encyclopedia Britannica.*
It's not a griffin, I said, *but maybe
a horned Pegasus, or a winged unicorn,
or a portmanteau—unipeg or pegacorn.*

        It's my fuckin' tattoo!
he yelled, punching the wall, and that was that
until the next trip, when he arrived with a parrot
on his chest. By then, I don't question species.

The next one was in my honour,
he said, my name inked in fancy script
on his lower left forearm.
My immediate thought?
*You'll be really sorry about that one
someday.*

29

⟩⟩⟩⟩● Slow Pitch

Jade's the new girl at work, twenty
to my twenty-two. She's been car-shopping,
asks what I like better, Trans Ams or Camaros.
Trans Ams, I shrug, not knowing the difference.

The following week, she invites me out
for a ride in her new glacier blue TA,
opens the door for me, offers me
driving lessons any time.

Later, she picks me up at home
to head to the ballpark. I'm the pitcher
for our Department of Supply and Services slow pitch team—
Public Serpents lettered large and white
across the back of our tight red scoop-neck t-shirts,
my nickname, *Belle,* in soft-flocked black print
above my left breast.

Always the innuendoes on the evening ball diamonds
about what we young women, all in our twenties,
should supply; who we should service
on the mostly male teams
from other government department offices
we played against. I liked nothing better
than to strike them out.

All through the season, Jade drives me
the long way home, talking about nothing
much, until the evening she slides
her hand across my thigh, parks
in front of my house.
> *Can I come in?* she asks.
> *I know your husband's at sea*
> *and I'd love to pinch-hit.*

⟩⟩⟩⟩●Wrong Reasons

Because we met in Halifax
Because I was eighteen
Because he was a sailor and I was a Naval Reservist
Because he wrote me letters after I went back home to Saskatoon
Because I was in first-year university
Because he lived in Victoria
Because the Navy posted me to Victoria the next summer
Because I was twenty
Because I thought he was cute
Because I was a thousand miles from home
Because I wanted to prove I could live my own life
Because we'd already moved in together
Because I didn't want my family to know I was living in sin
Because all my friends were marrying and drifting away
Because I was an island

Because he proposed
Because I thought no one else would ever want me
Because marriage would fix what wasn't right—
Because I was wrong.

⟩⟩⟩⟩● Bad Girl

Suppose you're five, and Mom says, *It's bad to let anyone see you naked*,
but you get sick, and Mom says, *Except for me and the doctor*,
and you keep getting sicker, and Mom takes you to Emergency,
and says, *Except for me and the doctor and nurse.*

Suppose you're six, and you point down below your belly,
and Mom says, *No one's supposed to touch you there*,
but the older neighbour boy says, *Let's play doctor, and you be a nurse.*
Later, he says, *It's a secret you can't tell because you're a naughty girl,
and you're very, very bad.*

Suppose your Grade 1 teacher is a nun and says, *Bad little girls will burn
in hell*, and you remember how much it hurt when you burned your hand
on the stove. Burning scares you, and you raise your hand for permission
to go to the bathroom, but she says, *No, so you pee through your panties*
and tights, and she slaps you, calls you *bad little girl.*

Suppose your Grade 7 teacher is also the principal, which means man,
and he also teaches sex education. He says, *Any of you can come ask me
anything in private anytime*, so you gather a few classmates together
after school and ask him to explain wet dreams. Afterwards, you laugh
hysterically with your friends about his embarrassment.
You're such a bad girl.

Suppose you're sixteen, double-dating with your boyfriend
at the drive-in. His best friend and his girlfriend are all too soon
fucking in the back seat, so your boyfriend coaxes your head
into his lap, forces himself into your mouth, moves your head
up and down, moans, *You're doing good, you bad bad girl.*

Suppose you're twenty, and you agree to get married, mostly because
all your friends are, and it seems to be the thing to do.
Suppose your husband insists you be *a slut in the sheets, but a lady
in the streets.* Suppose you bristle and seethe about his expectations.
Suppose your own desires lead a different direction.

PHASES

Suppose you finally say, *I'm my own person.*
Suppose you say, *No one else is in charge of me.*
Suppose you tell yourself, *I'm nobody's bad girl.*
Suppose you're that kind of woman. Just suppose.

⟩⟩⟩⟩● Midway

Gut-burning plunge, screaming,
the whiplash turns, twists,
and camel hoops—

the wooden rollercoaster
I'm trapped in, pulse
pounding, derailed.

I gasp awake—
relieved I'm not twenty-one
anymore, not still married

to the guy who secretly contracted
a full set of *Encyclopedia Britannica*
at the PNE ShowMart

and a nineteen-piece set
of Lifetime Regal Ware pots
and pans, five-ply stainless steel—

     Warranted forever, he cajoled
when I fretted about the monthly cost—
     nothing but the best for me,

pushed into the trap: cook, cleaner,
launderer, grocery shopper, bill payer,
social organizer, and apologizer
when he insulted co-workers, friends, family,

and me. His smooth talk decked me
in halter-top dresses, rubies, sapphires,
and diamonds we couldn't afford

despite my two jobs, despite
me knowing I would someday leave him
the hardcover volumes
to have and to hold.

⟩⟩⟩⟩● Right Reasons

Because he quit the Navy
Because he kept getting fired from every new job
Because he did nothing at home
Because I worked two jobs
Because he didn't like my friends
Because my friends didn't like him
Because he wouldn't cut up his credit cards
Because there was a recession
Because we moved
Because he got work in my hometown
Because he still kept getting fired
Because I worked two jobs again
Because I was tired
Because my family didn't like him
Because I didn't like him

Because he was twenty-seven
Because he was hanging out with teenage girls
Because I was twenty-four
Because I was done.

2

Grazing Occultation

*Masculine and feminine roles are not biologically fixed
but socially constructed.*
Judith Butler

))))●Bread

Sparrows flit, search
the browning grass. I watch
from the kitchen window—
millet, niger, flax seeds
scattered from the feeder
by the swing of the wind.
>   *Unlike you,*
>   he says, *those birds—*
>   *they know where*
>   *their bread is buttered.*

They're sparrows,
I say, *and the idiom is*
know which side
your bread is buttered on.

How foolish to speak
out loud, forgetting to duck
his fist, my ears ringing, eyes
swelling, him shouting,
>   *Who's the idiot now?*
>   and, *How many times*
>   *have I told you I don't give a damn*
>   *what you call them, they're just birds?*

I hear song
sparrows, goldfinches,
and chickadees—

they flock
to my rescue, beating
their glorious wings.

))))● Nothing Rhymes with Orange

It's always best
before the memories flood back—

all the times I sensed
a whiff of singed orange peels,
a psychic scent
that meant abuse—

the weaponry
of men's bodies.

No rescue from a knight
in shining armour,
no fairy godmother,
no guardian angel—

all my could-be saviours
watching me fall.

))))● **Shelter**

Three young men approach
from the dark, elbow and jostle
each other the night I stand
alone in the bus shelter.

I should cross back
to the hospital's lit doors—
but they shove in, knock me to the ground,

and I fear the worst
but I won't just let it happen
this time.
I scream, kick, swear, and roar.

They drag me out
and down the sidewalk,
wrestling for my shoulder bag
as I yell, *You fuckers!*,
until the final yank,
when they run off,

laughing, swinging
my purse. I don't cry
until I race back
inside the hospital doors,
back to shelter,

back to bright lights.

))))●Flight Path

I fill my pockets
with cold, smooth stones,
pick up my walking pole,
step onto crackled edges
of ice-skimmed water,

walk.

I break through, frigid
water, sink to the bottom—

look up to faraway moon shiver
beyond fish gleam
and airplane glint.

I could pierce them
with the sharp end of my stick,

watch people and roe
spill out from the underbellies
of silver fish.

⟩⟩⟩⟩● Personal Ad

It's the eighties, my cousin says,
and it's quite respectable now
to place a newspaper ad
looking for a good man.

She works the reception desk
at the *Star-Phoenix*, scrutinizes
the men who hand-deliver letters
to my confidential box number,

where I pick up
their handwritten replies, hear
whom she thought looked suitable.

I analyze their handwriting,
narrow my selection,
set up a half-dozen coffee dates
in safe public places.

One date becomes many
with a full-time single dad
of two pre-school children.

At thirty-two, I believe
I've finally got it right.
As instant as oatmeal and vanilla pudding,
I'm a mom—
married with children.

﹥﹥﹥﹥● The Rest is History

Those apples—no good for eating,
our new neighbour says
over the fence, tells me
how many other trees
the woman before me
had loved—Russian Olives, Little Leaf
Lindens, Tower Poplars, and Weeping
Birches, until the last screaming fight
when her husband chainsawed
them all, left her

only one ornamental
crabapple tree against
the back fence.

Years later, anger roars in my ears
as I speculate about the other woman,
contemplate my reasons to leave,

but my daughter finds me lying
where I've finally settled beneath the tree.

May sunshine wavers
through pale apple blossoms
as she gathers petals
to cover me—
and so I stay.

⟩⟩⟩⟩⟩● Siblings

My daughter rinses and tears
lettuce leaves, slices carrots and celery,

while her brother peels potatoes, grumbles,
　　High-school guys shouldn't have to
　　help make supper—
　　girls' work.

She says, *You know how to eat it,*
so learn how to make it.

He mimics her, falsetto voice:
　　None of my friends
　　have to do this.

She glares, hisses,
They should learn
to live in the real world,
think with their big head,
not their little one,

and his back stiffens
as he gouges a potato,
stabs an eye,

and then she says,
Watch this,

slices the knife hard
and fast—
the cucumber
cut in half.

⟩⟩⟩⟩● Understanding Hysterectomy

1. Pelvic Ultrasound

I'm in a darkened room
on an X-ray table—
a technician turns
the monitor toward me.

Latex-gloved, her hand
slathers cold gel
on my abdomen, slides
a black paddle, points a finger
at the screen—
images aquiver
in liquid light.

Her paddle pauses,
then stops. She looks directly
at me for the first time, asks,
> *Do you know why
> you were sent here?*

What can I say?
That bulky shape on the screen—
the crash of my heart.

2.   How Many Weeks

Round-bellied women
stare out the waiting-
room window, frown
at the wall clock, watch
each time a clerk picks
a chart, calls out a name.

Beside me, a woman caresses
the globe beneath her breasts,

dialect of hands—
mother to unborn child.

My hands are still.
Two hours later, my co-worker,
now my gynecologist,
sketches and points, says,
          Here and here, tumours—
          fibroids.
I feel hysteria's push—
bitter in my throat.

She slides a pamphlet
across her desk,
Understanding Hysterectomy,
as she urges me to sign
the consent form for surgery.

I stare at the wall—
poster of a fetus
in a womb, week-to-week,
as it grows to term.

I hesitate, request alternatives.
          There are none, she says.
          The biggest growth is too large.
I swallow hard.
How large? I ask.

She follows my gaze
to the wall, points—
          Twenty weeks.

3.   Hysterectomy Research

The librarian scans
my book selections
at the checkout counter.

          Research paper? she asks.
Sudden tears in my eyes
as I turn from her desk,
rush to the exit door.

Books tower beside my recliner
as I read, re-read,
dread the coming weeks.

A friend tells me
she'd gladly switch places—
          Take it all out, she says,
          that's what I'd tell them—
          wear white any day, no accident,
          no curse.

She can't understand
why I'm grieving
the imminent end of womb cycles—
upcoming separation
between me and the moon.

The night before surgery—
aching cramps,
sudden flow: blood
lets go one last time.

4.   Fruit Basket

And blessed is the fruit
of thy womb . . . Jesus.

In a mature woman,
a healthy womb
is the size of a pear.

Are my ovaries
as big as apricots?
Or maybe plums?

Pears should be left to ripen
at room temperature.
Apricots and plums also.

Fibroids are tumours—
small as berries or as large
as grapefruits, melons.

Thump melons lightly with the heel
of your hand—a ripe melon
sounds hollow.

In my blood basket
of mutated fruit:
spongy melons, mushy
with wasted seeds, wine-dark
plums, over-ripe apricots,
a bruised pear.

Requests to my surgeon:
A sharp scalpel.
Cut a straight line,
please. Leave me a plum.

5.   But What Did She Say?

I sit alone in the holding area
outside the O.R.—
no one to hold me.

I grip the underside
of the chair, almost crying.

I'm led to the theatre—single
white sheet on the operating table.
I obey instructions—step up
on the footstool, sit on the table
edge, lie down—
nowhere to run.

The anesthetist's soft guidance:
          Imagine lying on white sand.
          Warm sun, ocean waves lapping . . .

I choke awake—
saltwater waves
of nausea, sand in my throat.
A woman's soothing voice,
          Try to sleep.

Vague drift, uneasy doze,
remembering my gyne surgeon
spoke to me in the recovery room—
but what did she say?

6.   Patient-Controlled Analgesia

My name, repeated
close to my ear, cotton-
gauze voice—
          Everything went well.
          Do you feel any pain?

No, I feel good—
amazed to realize
it's true as I drift off,
wake again to my name, déjà vu.
          Do you feel any pain?

Each time I wake, I'm groggy
but feel okay. A nurse rechecks
my morphine pump—
          You haven't taken any yet—
          go ahead, use the pump.
          You don't have to act brave.

But it's a dawning awareness:
post-operative pain
doesn't compare to before—
it's relative bliss.

7.   The Day After

My surgeon checks in on me,
asks how I'm feeling. *Surprisingly okay,*
I reply, *but what did you tell me*
In the recovery room last night?

> *You'll be fine, but what a surprise.*
> *Your largest fibroid was so big*
> *we sent it to pathology in a pail.*
> *But all your fibroids are benign,*
> *and no other abnormalities noted*
>
> *other than the largest fibroid*
> *had shrunk since your laparoscopy*
> *last month. When I cut you open*
> *it was already dying, shrinking*
> *from lack of blood supply.*
> *Your body had quit feeding it.*

Maybe I didn't really need the surgery, then?

> *Oh, no, you did—it was still big enough*
> *it had to come out.*

She moves to the low wide windowsill,
inspects the flameless candle
centred among gemstones
arranged on embroidered cloth.
She smooths the tumbled amethysts
and moonstones in her hands, examines
the agate slice's almost invisible seam
of repair, pulls a rose quartz
from her pocket to add to my altar.

8.   Post-Operative—First Day

Awakening again, I touch the surgical staples—
a straight track from my navel to shaved pubis,

my stomach flat.
I struggle to sit up
but a white rabbit hinders me, plush
in the curve of my arm, a get-well card
tucked in alongside. Friends arrive, read me poems
and stories, but my eyes won't stay open.

When my daughter and husband appear,
he takes off his hat, slides the brim of his felt fedora 'round
and 'round through his fingers.

My daughter admires the gemstones and bouquets, breathes
in the scents from my friends, co-workers, and mother; chats
about her Grade 8 debate competition
as my eyes flutter close, but then she screams,

I'm bleeding! and my eyes startle open—blood gushes
from her nose, but my husband doesn't move, expects me
to take care of it as I've always done. She's sobbing
but I can't get out of bed to help her. I tell him,
*Take her to my bathroom sink, then get some ice
from the patients' kitchen,* while I try to calm her, remind her
to keep her head forward over the sink, pinch the bridge
of her nose like the nurse showed her last time
I took her to Emergency.

Her father returns, ice in the facecloth he hands to her—
sits again in the chair, turns his hat
like a wheel. Mentally, I hurl curses at him
while she coughs blood and tears, presses
the icy facecloth against her nose, but the flood
won't stop, and I direct him to take her to Emergency,
which makes her cry even harder.

Several hours later, my husband says he's wiped out,
but the pale and shaky ones are my daughter and me.
She insists on helping me out of bed, supports me
as I struggle to stand, holds my hand like she used to
on my slow, painful walk to the elevator
where we say goodbye.

She pinches the bridge of her nose
again, grips an ER bag of gauze squares.

All night I worry
about her
and the blood-spotted pad
between my thighs.

9.   Post-Op—Second Day

My abdomen distends—
an inflated balloon.

Staples rise—
an elevated railway track.

What's left
when something's taken out?

A silo cleared of grain.
A deserted robin's nest, broken
bits of blue on the earth below.
A stacking doll—
empty.

The nurse listens with a stethoscope
to my stomach, says there are no gut sounds
yet. She can't give me solid food
until my stomach makes noise—
proof it's working again
after anaesthetic.

Of course, I'm quiet
inside—scraped out
and hollow—
dark of the moon.

10. Back Home

Every bump in the road,
every train track we cross,
every icy rut, every stop and start
on the way home
makes me moan.
My incision so painful
I wonder, *Will the staples
really hold me together?*

I'm exhausted, need to rest,
but can't even manoeuvre myself
into our waterbed.
I move downstairs
to the guest bedroom
for my convalescence.

I like it down there—
sitting up in bed, drinking tea, reading
and writing poems—
sleeping alone.

⟩⟩⟩⟩● Lesbian Friends

Friends help out after surgery,
bring casseroles and baking,
do laundry, pitch in
to hire weekly maid services,
help me up the stairs,
make chai tea, visit
through the afternoons.

*Why do most of your friends
seem to be lesbians?* my husband asks.

*My friends are who they are.
They're strong, compassionate,
powerful, interesting women.
They're broad-minded feminists,
and we think alike.*

Interesting you say broad-minded.

*That's not a pun. Many of my friends
just happen to also be lesbians.
Would you rather
my friends were men?*

*Of course not,
it's just odd your women friends
are mostly gay.*

Mostly, I think
to myself,
so am I.

⟩⟩⟩⟩● Marriage Counselling (He Said, I Said)

Him: *Well?*
Me:
Him: *Well??*
Me: *I can't answer when you won't ask a sensible question.*

Counsellor: *What's one simple thing you both like
                that you can do together?*

Him: *Can I think about that for a bit? I might have to get back
         to you on that one.*

Me: *How about a walk—just a walk around the block?*

Him: *You walk too slow, want to look at every little thing—
         those shrubs, that flower bed, the moon rising
         over the rooftops. Or you walk too fast, like you're still at work
         racing hospital hallways, always a damn emergency.*

Me: *Maybe I should just walk and keep on walking.*

)))) Constant Craving
(after k.d. lang)

My husband and children
surround me as I unwrap
birthday gifts, a portable CD player,
and *Ingenue*, k.d. lang's newest recording.

Her voice and lyrics illuminate
my darkest phases. An inner magnet
pulls me to parenthood, to the two children
I love fiercely, but not their dad.

I'm a full-time stepmom.
How can I leave?
Leaving him would mean
leaving them.

Alone at home, I play the song
on repeat, sobbing. I know now
what my constant craving
has always been—

to accept what I've never dared
admit to myself before, to be
who I really am beneath my skin—
a lesbian.

3

Perigee Syzygy

Don't try to comprehend with your mind. Use your intuition.
Madeleine L'Engle

Poems are like dreams: in them, you put what you don't know you know.
Adrienne Rich

I am out with lanterns, looking for myself.
Emily Dickinson

⟩⟩⟩⟩● Where There is Darkness

I'm out of control, something
only an owl knows, tiny heart
beats under the snow, crystalline.

Nightfall.
Life has undone me.

What's left is moon
gliding across a dance floor,
maple hardwood over horsehair, buoyant.

Lake water, melt
edged with sand and foam.
Shadows meet me, merge
into skin.

White wings beat at glass.
It's death I'm defying—
light flailing.

)))))● **Soundless**

Feathers drift
from my hair this morning—
proof I flew
last night.

Talons tore flesh,

dismembering.

Skulls slept with rocks, cradled
in moss and leaves—
the moon high-strung.

Let the bones dream
for me—

bright belt of stars
across the night's sway of hips.

⟩⟩⟩⟩● To the Bonehouse

It's where you say
we all go eventually,

whether flesh or feather, our bones
dense or hollow,

no matter if we fly on wings
or a prayer.

Angels billow from clouds
overhead. Leaves wither, drift
to the earth.

Wide-winged shadows glide
soundless through the aspens—
owls on a night hunt—

while we women light candles
outside the crematorium.

Chanting to the moon,
we pace slowly through
the labyrinth.

〉〉〉〉● **Tombstone Dealers**

Side by side, gravestone
companies compete
along the street leading
into Woodlawn Cemetery.

I park outside the gates, walk past
square stone pillars that mark
the entrance to Next of Kin Avenue—

roadway soldiered by elms and oaks
and plaques wrought in iron—
one for the Unremembered Boys, dedicated
by a comrade, his surname indecipherable.

Outside the cemetery gates,
a crumbling bakery's boarded-up windows
and weathered sign
       fresh bread and buns daily
above it, a billboard
       the best dough in town
graffiti sprayed over in red—

       Fee-Fi-Fo-Fum.

PHASES

))))●Tsunami

Winter darkness breaks,
gives way to uncertain morning.

Mist gathers. Clouds billow
outside my window.

Flakes of snow double and redouble.
Grace unfolding, white-edged

in woven light. Trees glisten—
psalms murmured in a thin wind.

But from across the world, unfathomable news.
Oceans swell and heave,

surges of salt water, swift and roaring.
No magic circle keeps life from spilling.

Tentative evening. Shaken world.
Cascading prayers pour and overflow.

Deep sadness swirls against my window.
Ruined prayers float like feathers. Nothing is gold.

⟩⟩⟩⟩● Carrying the Moon

All the months I spent
with winter, hibiscus blossoms
faded and drooped, the moon
adrift on leaves frozen under ice, its eclipse
in the dim of waking dreams, the oracle of grief.

Carrying the moon in the palm
of my black gloves, the wind's swift clouds
blur, then clear, then smudge—
now wraith, now moon, now dark,

trains of thought whistling
through night drifts
of moonlight's haiku—

brilliance, then obscurity—
fresh falling snow.

⟩⟩⟩⟩● Vermin

When I startle awake,
the night's moonless body
scurries across my neck—
claws at my throat.

From the kitchen, the snap
of a trap—shriek
in the darkness.

When I catch my breath
again, I know I, too,
would choose escape—
chew off my own foot.

⟩⟩⟩⟩● Stations

Letters cross in the mail; cross words and accusations,
knitted brow and stunned silence.

This is a crossroad, a place of intersection.
Bless the little flower, its sign of the cross.

Thoughts cross-purposed—
light and shadow behind my eyes.

Connecting lines form patterns on paper.
Eliminate them. Cross them off my list.

Threads cross-stitched, undone, restitched.
Unravelling has its purpose.

I will cross over.

⟩⟩⟩⟩● Boundless

My hands
on the wheel,

music to drive to,
silence to drive away from.

I thought there was nothing
bigger than the sky, but there is:

all that light
I cannot hold.

⟩⟩⟩⟩● Perigee Syzygy

Full moon—
so large, so close—
outside my back door.

I lift my arms, stretch
my hands to its radiance—
ten moons
rise from my nail beds.

I turn my palms
toward me—
ten crescents
glow, translucent
above each fingertip.

I slide my hands
over bare breasts
to scarred belly
and lower—
the quickening inside.

››››● Single Woman and a Bear

A friend brings a housewarming gift—
a huge stuffed bear
to keep me company.

Plush and gentle, it nuzzles
into blankets, tucks
into my arms, snores
softly on my pillow.

Now that I'm single again,
I sleep easy—
bear snout at my neck,

its paws at my breasts
innocuous.

⟩⟩⟩⟩● Mating Dance

Pre-dawn light—
sharp-tailed grouse hunker down

in prairie grass. Cloudless sunrise
blazes through the window

as male grouse face off in pairs,
inches from each other.

Stock-still, wings drop at their sides,
white tails fan skyward,

purple-pink neck sacs inflate.
Suddenly, they pummel the ground,

jump at each other, kicking out—
jagged coos and cackles as they scurry

and dart while the females ignore them—
backs turned to the display.

Hours later, I sign a wedding guest registry,
hug friends at round tables

sprinkled with heart-shaped confetti.
After dinner and speeches

and glasses raised high, teen girls
in lace dresses and high heels

tap their feet to the music
while adolescent boys squirm

inside their suits, tug their ties,
jostle and shove as they pretend

not to notice the girls
pretending not to notice them.

But then the DJ amps up
"Old Time Rock and Roll,"

jackets and ties tossed aside,
high heels kicked off,

everyone's dancing—
thumping the floor.

⟩⟩⟩⟩● Wave Me Over (Peggy's Cove, November)

Blurred in thick fog fur,
we tug on gloves and hats, turn up collars.

I struggle with a new memory card,
slip the camera strap over my wrist,
take my first picture—a warning sign—
Keep Off the Black Rocks!

I wander away, hear women singing,
see their arms wave as they call,
        Come closer, come here.

Sunlight illuminates cratered rock,
translucent green waves smash
as the chorus persists, beckons,
        Come closer, come here,

and I take one step after another
onto wet black rocks.

From above and behind,
my friends shout,
        Come back, come here!

and I yell back,
*Just a few more pictures, just a few
more waves—*

whirled around, bashed to my knees,
churned and inhaling salt water, I gag
and gasp as I'm sucked along rock,
sliding offshore, but my right knee
slams into a fissure,
my fingers clutch crevices
as the last of the wave
slides off me, back to the sea,
and I freeze, shiver,
as my friends rush, yell, urge me
to get on hands and knees, crawl

toward them on dry rock,
where they pull me to safety, hurry me
to warmth inside the only open shop.

As I drip and shake at the counter,
the sales clerk shakes her head, says,
People like you die out there every year.

She leads me to a change room, hands in
a towel, a few sweatshirts and sweatpants, says,
We don't sell underwear, socks, or shoes.

I leave the gift shop in bare feet
and a souvenir outfit—
my drenched clothes and boots
double-bagged.

Later, I open my camera.
It's full of dried salt, but I test
my memory card in the laptop.

Photos appear in reverse—
the last wave towers
in front of me,
rising to the sun.

4

Orbital Eccentricity

We're born naked, and the rest is drag.
RuPaul

Drag wasn't always counterculture.
Joni Mitchell

⟩⟩⟩⟩● Pierce

The woman who pierces
flesh for a living
snaps blue rubber gloves
on her long, narrow hands,

arranges her instruments—
three silver needles
in sealed cellophane
scissor-handled clamp.
She positions cotton swabs
and alcohol, antibiotic soap.

No obvious expression,
no earrings, studded eyebrows
or tongue. She says,
> *I've had everything pierced—*
> *everything—and more*
> *than once.*
> *It's my addiction,*
> *an adrenalin rush—*
> *pain that proves I'm alive.*
>
> *And after the holes heal—*
> *I pierce myself again.*

She leans close, marks my skin,
asks which piercing
I want first.

The one that hurts most,
I say, and I hold my breath
while the first needle pushes
through and heat rushes in
and I breathe

breathe

to this place
of knowing.

75

››››●Once Upon a Time

Never the sweet-grained flesh
of a pear, plum's slick pulp,
or salacious pomegranate,
juicy and red, dripping
seeds through her fingers
as she faints
in the darkening forest.

Always
the god-
damned
apple.

Always that catch
in her throat.

Always asleep,
waiting for a kiss,

while bears and huntsmen
stalk the woodland.

But now, here come
the stepmothers and witches,
brides and butches,
with covered baskets—knives
up their sleeves.

⟩⟩⟩⟩● Not the F Word
(Gay Latté, Pride Week, Saskatoon)

The only word
I was asked not to use
was the F word.

No, not feminist, fruit, fag, fornicate,
that other F word.
No worries. I won't say it.
I also won't say screw, lay, nail,
hump, bang, ball,
do the wild thing, do night laps,
do the nasty, do the bone dance boogaloo—
I won't say get down, get it on,
get horizontal, get skronkin', get in the saddle.

I won't say dust my broom, peel me a grape,
butter the muffin, dive for pearls, sauce the clam,
gild the lily, shake the sheets.

I won't say
boff, diddle, bang, boink,
do you up, do you down, do the deed,
do the belly-to-belly,
get it up, get down,
get some, get to first base,
get a taste, get it together.

I won't say
jig jag, jing jang,
bump bones,
shake it down,
make it, make out,
put out, go all the way,
wing-ding,
ring one's bell—
wink, wink, nudge, nudge
if you know what I mean—
no, I won't say any of it.

Who needs the F word
when there's all the rest of the alphabet?

⟩⟩⟩⟩●Closets

I was never the kid
afraid of monsters
in my closet.

I knew what was behind
my bi-fold doors—
letters from pen pals in Montana, California,
and New Brunswick—
Dear Diary secret codes
scrawled in Hilroy notebooks,
tucked among art-class drawings
and A-plus assignments,

transferred from closet to cabinet
as I moved beyond childhood,
closer to my truth.

Now, it's just a cliché—
my closet is only for clothes.

〉〉〉〉● **Coming Out**

It's been months
since we worked together
but now we take a coffee-break
walk along the river. You ask me,
        What's new?
You're speechless
after my reply:

I've met someone—a woman.
September trees spill fire over water—
reflections waver. Finally, you say,
        But we can still be friends, right?

I stop in my tracks.
Yes, absolutely—I don't like you like THAT,
and after laughter, you ask,
        Which one of you plays the man?

I recall that classic routine–
Who's on first,
what's on second,
I don't know's on third—

but now, I'm playing
the outfield.

⟩⟩⟩⟩● What Do Lesbians Do?

An old friend asks me,
What do lesbians do?

I say, *We live*
in houses or condos or apartments,
we drive or walk or bike to work,
we shop for groceries and chardonnay,
we have potlucks and dinner parties,
we go to dances and the bar once in a while,
we like musicals and movies and live theatre and art shows—
pretty much just like everybody else.

She says, *Yeah, but, you know—*
that's not what I mean
you know—really—
what do lesbians do?

Well, then—
if you want the truth
we don't go out,
we don't do dinner, movies, or dates—
we frolic all day
and all night, we dive
into the pleasures
of each other's flesh,

we forget to eat,
except for each other,

savour the taste of ourselves
on each other's tongues—

our swollen lips.

⟩⟩⟩⟩● Not Just Dessert

Lovers of each other
    (not me, not mine)
visit over long winter evenings,
compose magnetic messages on my fridge:

women kiss delicious & hard
soft woman belly under my hand
woman, you are constant craving.

They hold hands, laughing, add a crossword to the mix:

above every moist woman is a tongue
                                    shower of
a thousand tongues wet fingers sweet
                shake   *woman*
                my   *pie*
                centre
lick lathered luscious lips
delicious moans

read it aloud to me as I stir
the gravy, slice the roast.

Many glasses of wine later,
arms around each other, words
in each other's ears, they leave
me. I clear the dessert plates—

lick mine clean, memory moist
with the taste of the first woman
who kissed me—
her winter mouth
against my summer skin.

⟩⟩⟩⟩●At the Gay Bar

I flirt with men, secure
in their own femininity
and comfortable with dykes.

I flirt with drag queens,
quick tongue-twisting sexual innuendoes—
their fake eyelashes flutter
as they stroke my thigh.

I flirt with women
like that one at the bar last night—
her shoulders back, slow scan
up and down, look-me-in-the-eyes
I-want-you-later gaze,

and you bet we watched
each other, aura
of quickening, acute
awareness of her dark
blue eyes, her wink, her grin.
It doesn't matter who followed who
to the ladies' room, corner stall—

I got her number
and she sure got mine.

PHASES

⟩⟩⟩⟩●Tick

Bright aftrnoon. T-shirts and shorts
scatter as we rush to your bed

but your phone interrupts, incessant
until you answer—your neighbour
has a tick she can't get out.

Over at her house, she leads us
to her bedroom, strips
off her cut-offs, lays back
on the bed, opens her legs—
the tick almost fully burrowed in.

Your face close to her skin, still-smoking
match a hair's breadth
against the tick's domed end,

your other hand with tweezers—
a quick yank, and it's out.

When you leave to flush
the tick away, she makes no move
to dress, instead spreads her thighs wider
asks me to kiss it all better—awkward
silence when you return.

After you and I go back
to your house, I wonder
whose thighs you're thinking of—
your urgent tongue's
circuitous route.

⟩⟩⟩⟩● Super Sexe (Montreal)

The guys from our health conference
said it was the best
peeler bar—they were straight
and thought we'd like the strippers.

The three of us self-declared dykes
walked to Rue Sainte-Catherine to flag
a cab, laughed when he drove
us just six blocks—he could've told us
we were that close. At the top

of the stairs. the bouncers ID'd us, looked
us up and down, made us wait
while they discussed whether to let lesbians
in their bar, while we conferred about leaving—
all those men shuffling behind us.

But then, a security guard ushered us
to a back table. Overcharging
us for a beer and two Cokes, the g-stringed
waitress refused to leave until we spilled
a better tip onto her tray. Two expressionless
strippers pole-danced, stroked
painfully long nails
across breasts and thighs, licked
each other's bald vulvas—

we couldn't escape fast enough
down the stairs and out to the street,
where we hurried away, small

cliques of women
in lacy party dresses
passing us by.

⟩⟩⟩⟩● A Man, Passing

So beastly hot
in Montreal, I walk
into the first barber shop I find
on Sainte-Catherine.

　　　Non, non, he says,
but unsure whether he means
women's cuts, or cutting women's hair, I mime
a clipper trimming close to my scalp.

He shrugs, leads me to the cracked black vinyl chair
by the window where the sun
scorches in, my eyes shut in the heat.

　　　J'ai fini, he says as he whips the dark cape
away from my brother's face
in the mirror—
Merci, monsieur
as I pay and leave.

Back at my hotel—
　　　Bonjour, monsieur say the doorman,
　　　the concierge, the housekeeper in the hallway.

At *Le Drugstore* gay bar that night,
it's men who ask me to dance—
like I'm one of them.

))))●Feast

After the heat
of the afternoon,

you swing your long legs
out of bed,

sway away from me
toward the kitchen, return

with sliced Ambrosia apples,
seedless green grapes,

and two glasses
of chilled Blue Mountain chardonnay.

We toast each other
eye to eye, and afterwards—

the warmth of you, your breasts
against my back,

breath slow and easy
on my neck.

⟩⟩⟩⟩● Moon Tongue

Your kiss,
delicious and hard—
a thousand broken stars.

Your scent—
hidden blossom of bare dark
roses, blush
of moon tongue.

This slow knife
longing—

lips on my lips—

your tongue
where I have none.

>>>>●**Street Corner**

Rusty old Datsun
stuffed full of guys,
staring and heckling
as we hold hands
at the intersection.

       Fuckin' dykes, they yell,
tires squealing
when the light changes.

I shout back, middle finger
thrust out—*Yeah, you're right,*
we do that
better than any guy.

⟩⟩⟩⟩● Folk Festival

Front and centre
at the raised outdoor stage,

I scream as loud
as the other lesbians and folkies
in the sea of summer hats,

but after years of playing
Indigo Girls disks on repeat
and lyrics seared into memory,

I can no longer call myself
their biggest fan—

the baby dyke beside me
has just revealed
her favourite phrase
from "Closer to Fine"

freshly tattooed
around her tender
young neck.

⟩⟩⟩⟩● Why a Parade?

For the four-year-old girl
who rejects her dolls and miniature ponies
for toy cars, trains, and Lego,

and the seven-year-old boy
who would rather skate
Lutz and Axel jumps
than play hockey,

and the twelve-year-old tomboy
who cries when her mother insists,
          It's time you wear a bra,

and the thirteen-year-old
who has less in common
with the guys than his girlfriends,

and the fourteen-year-old
who's bored with her friends
giggling about really cute guys,

and the eighteen-year-old boy
who obsesses about wanting
breasts and no penis,

and the twenty-five-year-old guy
lingering over the glossy pages
of *Men's Health,*

and the thirty-one-year-old
trans woman who doesn't know
how to tell her family she wants
sex reassignment surgery,

and the thirty-eight-year-old wife
who agonizes about how to leave
her husband for a younger woman,

and the forty-five-year-old husband
who cruises dark city parks
and for the men he hooks up with,

and the fifty-six-year-old widow
who discovers romantic love
with her longtime lady-friend,

and the sixty-two-year-old
pansexual who's in between
relationships,

and the seventy-four-year-old man
keeping a hospital vigil
for his friend and secret lover,

and the eighty-three-year-old
self-identified queer
and lifelong activist,

and the ninety-one-year-old
in a nursing home, afraid
to be out of the closet—

for all of them,
and all the others

who don't identify
with gender and sexual norms,
who don't fit the stereotypes, labels, and acronyms,
who are still discovering their true selves,

for all of them,
and all of us,
and all our allies—

that's why
a parade.

⟩⟩⟩⟩● Drag King

1.
Remember watching your first
drag show?

Drag queens—elegant
in elaborate outfits,

cleavage, bounce
and sashay, high heels, glittering
flash dance—then

the Drag King—

sideburns, goatee, confident
bulge in his crotch.

That's when the seed
was planted, something
that expanded your ribs, spread
across your shoulders, swelled

in your groin, that feeling
some days of being
different.

It's not clothes
that make a man

but your carriage, broad
shoulders, make you believe
you can pull it

off, the illusion—
passing as a man.

Don't think too much,
don't over-analyze

but you might, when you pass

through women's wear
to the men's department
in Value Village, Village Green
to try on hardly-worn suits—
wonder about the men
who shrugged them off.

Start questioning, asking
around, talking about drag.

If your girlfriend threatens,
          I'll leave if you start doing drag!
hide your smile.

All the more reason.

Don't worry about definitions,
identifiers, labels—
sex deviant, gender-anomalied dyke,
lesbian-identified boi,
non-operative female-bodied transgender outlaw,
genderbender, genderfucker, genderqueer.

Tonight, it's just you
and the mirror.

2.
Methods of gender illusion—
hide/bind breasts.
A small-breasted drag king succeeds
with layers of tight sports bras,

the full-breasted
resort to tensor bandages,
backward-worn back braces,
compression vests, duct tape—

Caution!
Binding with plastic food wrap
inhibits blood flow, constricts breathing.

Hairstyle—
butch cuts, buzz cuts, faux hawks.
Headcovers—
ball caps, tuques,
bowlers, snap-brim hats.

Packing—
what's your preference
for simulated phallus?
Socks, strap-on
manufactured bendie,
half an apple?

Whatever you use, make sure
it's good and tight.
You don't want
to lose it.

Now you know
why some guys grab
themselves.

Naming—
a memorable, unique drag
name is essential.

Be macho, sexual,
playful—your name must embody
your persona, self-image,
and sense of humour

but don't call yourself
Cass Butchity, Ben Dover, Flip Dover,
Manny Nuff, Dixon Deep,
Mr. Layher, Mr. E—

like all good men,
they're already
taken.

PHASES

Attitude—
men move differently in the world.
Swagger, don't sway.

Practice, practice
in front of a full-length mirror.
Practice how you walk, stand, sit,
angle your head. Perform
decisive, crisp movements.

Have your best gay buddy
evaluate your performance.
He's obsessive about watching
men, can give you pointers—
how to move, walk, dance
like a macho guy.

Take it to the next step.
At the gay bar, be out
in face.

Look evenly at everyone.
Never lower your eyes—
no coy sideways glances
unless you're on the receiving end.

Sit with your knees wide open.
Hold your cigarette with fingers slightly bent,
draw deep, exhale smoke rings.
Flick, don't tap.

Stand with arms crossed,
one leg cocked,
back against the wall
when you're checking out
a woman.

Walk loose, take up space
like you own it.

Sling your thumbs
through your front belt loops,
fingers pointing
at your crotch.

Be cocky
with the women and queens.
Be bold, ballsy,

act as if
you own the world, as if
the world owes you.

Next time, project
a different personality.
Be a gentleman—
hold doors open
for the ladies, let them
go first.

Light their cigarettes
with your own fire.

Take it up
a notch.

Sign up
for the next drag show
at the club.

Rehearse lip-synching
at home, in your car—
play tracks over and over.

Memorize songs that fit
varied aspects of your characters—
storyteller, troubadour, crooner, hard
rocker, pop star.

Master
lyrics and timing
for each new song.

Emphasize the movement
of your mouth, but don't
over-accentuate—
that's for queens.

Rehearse at home, repeat
dry run, repeat, run through.

Check your look
in the mirror—
go over and over
your new song and dance.

Performance night—
when your number
cues up, breathe
deep, launch yourself
onstage with bravado.

Play up to the women
and men—
they love it.
lap it
up.

Collect your tips
gallantly, savour
their compliments.

Tonight, it's just you
and them.

3.
Build your reputation.
Develop your repertoire
of characters—a bad boy
in plaid, frank and bold—

effeminate flamer, swishy
walk and fuchsia scarf—

suave crooner, gentleman
in suit, tie, and snap-brim hat—
comedian with a funny song
and goof-ball
act. Show off.

Sass the audience.
Once in a while,
drop your pants, flash
your heart-patterned boxers—

you'll always get
a roar of appreciation
from the crowd.

Expand
your community, develop
your chosen family.
Involve your drag mama, drag brothers,
in your acts. Create your own
family history.

Hang out
between sets
outside the club—
performers
and audience, all
on their own highs.

At closing time, bask
in the camaraderie
backstage. Join the smokers
in the alley—
the aftershow glow.

When someone wants you
to take them home,

ask yourself how
they identify—
female? male? trans? gay? bi?

straight? swinger?
top, bottom, or switch?
chocolate or vanilla?
anything that moves?

How do they imagine
sex will play out?

How do you?

Keep them guessing.
Keep it under
your hat.

Your balls
in your court—
you call the shots.

Take yourself
home. Tonight,
you know
who you are.

Tonight,

it's just
you.

⟩⟩⟩⟩● Ask a Drag King

What drew you to drag?

Gender play fucking with gender
getting fucked like the straight guys getting the girls
for the fame for the title for the rush
because it scares the hell out of me
to challenge myself to entertain to swagger
to make people laugh make them think
make them feel make me feel
to get in touch with my masculine side
to reconnect to my feminine side
to have pockets to not need a purse
to feel power
to feel safe.

⟩⟩⟩⟩● In Drag

What possesses me
to cut clippings of my hair,
chop them finer with manicure scissors,
save them in a clear pill bottle
in my medicine cabinet?

What possesses me
on Saturday night
to gaze in the mirror—
darken my eyebrows with mascara,
glue hair clippings into the shape
of sideburns, moustache, goatee?

What possesses me
to bind my breasts,
put on a man's shirt, tie, and suit,
top it all off
with the '50s snap-brim hat
my father wore before I was born?

What possesses me
to strut down the alley
to the gay bar, stroll on stage
to lip-sync popular new versions
of old jazz standards?

What possesses me
is them—
cheering and whistling,
begging for more—
gay, trans, straight,

shouting out
they love me.

⟩⟩⟩⟩● Texting Dyke van Dick

1.

      Dyke van Dick, Dick Van Dyke—is it any wonder
      people mix up your name? How about DVD for short?
Hmmm, a DVD is something you push in to play—
I see what you're getting at :)

2.

      Clever name for a drag king, but can I just call you Dyke?
      You're a lesbian, right?
Ah yes, what's in a name—
yes, and yes, you can call me Dyke.

3.

      I'd like to get to know you better—a lot better ;) Call me!
Meet me in the alley after the next show—
wear a red rose in your hair, so I'll know it's you.

4.

      Why do you do what you do? I don't get it.
If you don't get it, why do you keep coming
back to the drag shows?

5.

      You don't fool anyone with that glued-on facial hair—
      just quit it already!
Can't stop this thing I've started—

6.

      What do you wear under your plaid shirt and carpenter jeans?
Underwear ;)!

7.

      I love that you do what you do—you can do me any time!
Thanks! Meet me in the alley—take a number.

8.

      I'll show you mine if you show me yours—
It's Showtime!

〉〉〉〉● **The Right Woman**

Ask her out to a drag show.
Be in drag to go pick her up.

If she smiles when she opens the door,
you're off to a good start.

Introduce her to your drag family at the bar.
Gauge her reaction to them, their reaction to her.

When the floor clears after you finish
your last number in the show, invite her to dance.

If it's a slow song, hold her close—
don't even talk, just move with the music.

When you go to get her a drink, and your friends say
        she never took her eyes off you the whole show—

let that sink in. You're intrigued,
and the night's getting late.

Let her know you'll take her home
when she's ready to leave. Let her know

you mean your home. If she keeps smiling
and hugs you hard, you know she's the one.

Marry the woman who loves you—
in and out of drag.

Notes

Caveat: it would be incorrect to assume all of these poems are strictly autobiographical. That said, some of them are.

The title "A Doctor Talks to 9-to-12-year-olds" is from the paperback booklet of the same name, by Marion O. Lerrigo, Ph.D. in consultation with Michael A. Cassidy, M.D., Budlong Press Company, 1967.

"Coming Out" references a classic vaudeville routine popularized by the comedy team Abbott and Costello in the late 1930's. "Who's on First" became famous after its inclusion in the 1945 film *The Naughty Nineties.*

"Super Sexe" was an iconic strip club in Montreal from 1978 to 2017.

Le Drugstore referenced in "A Man, Passing" was a three-storey nightclub in Montreal's Gay Village. It had six levels and four outdoor terraces. It closed in 2013.

Acknowledgements

Earlier versions of some of these poems first appeared in the anthologies *Fast Forward: New Saskatchewan Poets* and *Within These Lines*; the journals *spring Vol. 7*, *spring Vol. 9*, and *The Society 2015*; and the chapbooks *Food Works: Plums in the Icebox*, *Out of Our Depth*, and *Where Dragonflies Go*. Other poems were performed at queer-themed presentations: Queer Showcase—Canadian National Festival of Spoken Word; Saskatoon's EYAO Queer Arts Festivals; Gay Latté; and the live video presentation "Write It Out—Writing with Pride" for the Saskatchewan Writers' Guild, June 2019.

Many thanks to the provincial and local organizations who support and promote writers, especially the Saskatchewan Writers' Guild, Sage Hill Writing, and the Saskatoon Public Library Writer in Residence program.

I'm above and beyond grateful for past and present members of my writing groups: Sisters' Ink; The Obsessors; and Write & Read; especially Cindy Clarke, Lori Ulrich, Carla Roppel, Dianne Miller, Katherine Lawrence, Bronwen McRae, Holly Keeler, Leanne Boyce, Gary Chappell, Mic LaFreniere, Lou Erickson, Jocelyne Doucet, and Joan Falk.

To Dave Margoshes—you know I'll thank you forever because I can't thank you enough!

Heartfelt thanks to Liz Phillips, Sandra Ridley, Sylvia Legris, Katherine Lawrence, and Beth Goobie for guidance and encouragement, and to Jeanette Lynes for her graciousness.

Kisses and a tip of my snap-brim hat to my drag family, particularly my Brovers/brothers Ben Dover and Flip Dover, and my drag Mama, Crystal Clear; and to Kelly Faber, who owned and operated Divas in Saskatoon and provided a supportive home for our drag community before, during, and after my reign as Mr. Diva's 2005/Mr. Gay Saskatoon 8.

Huge thanks to Barbara Klar and John Barton for inspiration and motivation during the early stages of this book and for their enthusiastic support of Drag King.

High fives to the Octopi group and Sage Hillers who cheered the drag poems, especially Eufemia Fantetti.

Gratitude for the first edition of this book to John, Mazin, and Susan of Coteau Books; and editor Tracy Hamon.

Extra special thanks to Edward Willett of Shadowpaw Press for adopting *Phases* and giving it new life in this expanded and revised second edition.

I am fortunate to have family who have inspired and championed me—birth family, extended family, chosen family, LGBTQ2S+ family, drag family, and literary family. Love and thanks to all my families—in more ways than you know, you've all inspired my writing and my life.

Most of all, love and gratefulness always to: my Mom for everything (and for giving me Dad's snap-brim hat); to tessera for balance and wisdom; to Ashley and Ryan for cheerfulness and enthusiasm; and to my wife Beth, the love of my life, for always supporting and believing in me.

About the Author

Belinda Betker
Photo by Heather Brenneman

Dyke van Dick
Photo by Debra Marshall

Belinda Betker (aka Dyke Van Dick) is a prairie-born poet living in Saskatoon with her Australian wife and their rescue dog, a springer-spaniel/terrier cross. The first edition of this poetry collection was a 2020 finalist for two Saskatchewan Book Awards.

Belinda's poetry and award-winning haiku are also published on-line and in various anthologies, literary journals, and chapbooks.

Belinda is a founding member of two long-running Saskatoon writing groups, Sisters' Ink and The Obsessors. She was also a founding and longtime board member of the Saskatoon Writers' Collective.

ALSO AVAILABLE FROM

SHADOWPAW
PRESS *Premiere*

Thickwood
By Gayle M. Smith

The Emir's Falcon
By Matthew Hughes

What if You Could?
By Lynne Harley

One Lucky Devil
The First World War Memoirs of Sampson J. Goodfellow
By Sampson J. Goodfellow

Paths to the Stars
Twenty-Two Fantastical Tales of Imagination
By Edward Willett

Shapers of Worlds
Shapers of Worlds Volume II
Shapers of Worlds Volume III
Science fiction and fantasy by authors
who were guests on the award-winning podcast
The Worldshapers

Star Song
by Edward Willett